How
your body
works

What happens
when you
eat?

Jacqui Bailey

WAYLAND

First published in 2007
by Wayland

Wayland
338 Euston Road
London NW1 3BH

Wayland Australia
Level 17/207 Kent Street
Sydney NSW 2000

Senior Editor: Jennifer Schofield
Consultant: Dr Patricia Macnair
Designer: Phipps Design
Illustrator: Ian Thompson
Picture Researcher: Kathy Lockley
Proofreader: Susie Brooks

Picture acknowledgements
Paul Doyle/Alamy Images: 6; Russell Glenister/image 100/Corbis: Cover
Tim Hill/Alamy Images: 14; Tony Heald/Nature Picture Library: 9
Maximilian Stock Ltd/Jupiterimages: 7; Fritz Polking/Still Pictures: 25t
Turbo/zefa/Corbis: 21t; Wayland Archive: 11, 18, 17, 20, 21b, 23, 24, 25b, 26, 27t

CIP data
Bailey, Jacqui
   What happens when we eat? - (How does your body work?)
   1. Digestive organs - Juvenile literature
   I. Title
   612.3

ISBN: 978 0 7502 5130 3

Printed in China

Wayland is a division of Hachette Children's Books.

Contents

Why do we eat?

We eat food to give us energy and to keep our bodies working properly.

Your body uses energy all the time, even when you sleep. You use energy to run and jump and move around, and also when you breathe, when your heart beats and to keep your body warm. Food also helps your body to grow and repair itself when it is damaged, and helps your body to fight off illnesses.

Your body uses different types of food in different ways. The mixture of foods you eat is known as your diet. When you eat a good mixture, you have a balanced diet.

Just as a car stops moving when it runs out of fuel, your body would eventually run out of energy and stop working if you did not eat.

If you do not eat enough of some foods, or too much of others, you may have an unbalanced diet. An unbalanced diet is bad for your health.

How much food you need depends on your size and how active you are. Small children need less food than teenagers and adults. If you are active and use lots of energy you need to eat lots of food to replace that energy. If you do less exercise and use less energy, your body needs less food.

Your body uses different foods in different ways, so you need to eat a mixture of foods every day.

What makes a meal?

All animals need to eat, but we do not all need the same types of food. Cows and horses live on a diet of grass and hay, but dogs, cats or humans would become very ill if they tried to do the same thing.

Where does the food go?

Before your body can make use of the food you eat, the food has to be digested. This means the food is broken up into tiny pieces.

Breaking up food allows your body to separate the good bits, called nutrients, from the bits that it does not need, called waste matter. Digestion starts the minute you put a piece of food into your mouth and can last for up to 24 hours, depending on what you eat.

All the parts of your body that help to break up food belong to the digestive system.

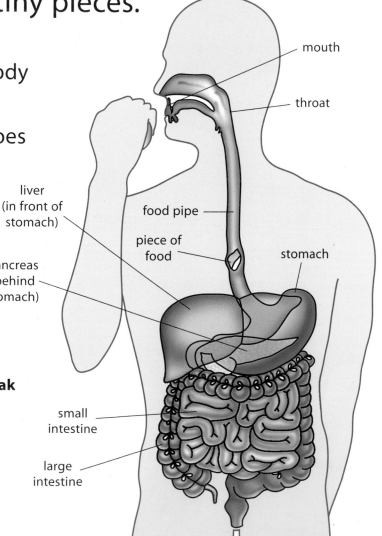

mouth

throat

liver
(in front of
stomach)

food pipe

piece of
food

stomach

pancreas
(behind
stomach)

small
intestine

large
intestine

8

Your digestive system is a very long tube that is divided into different stages. It leads from your mouth to your stomach and then from your stomach to your bottom. In some places it is straight and quite narrow. In others it is bag-like, or folded up like a string of sausages.

As food travels through the digestive tube, other parts of your body, such as your mouth, liver and pancreas, put liquids into the tube. The liquids help to soften and break down the food. All these parts of the body belong to the digestive system.

If you laid out your digestive tube in a straight line it would stretch for eight metres – that is almost as long as two elephants standing face to face.

See for yourself

Find a ball of wool and a tape measure. Measure out a piece of wool that is eight metres long. This is roughly how long your digestive tube is.

Biting and chewing

Digestion starts with your mouth. A lot of things happen in your mouth when you put food into it.

If the food is hard, you use your teeth to bite and chew it. Open your mouth wide and have a look at your teeth in a mirror. Can you see that your teeth have different shapes? The ones at the front are squarish with flat edges. They are called incisors. These are your cutting teeth. You use them for slicing chunks out of big pieces of food.

On each side of the incisors, top and bottom, is a sharper, more pointed tooth. These are the four canine teeth. You use these for stabbing and tearing a mouthful from food that is tough and chewy, such as a piece of meat.

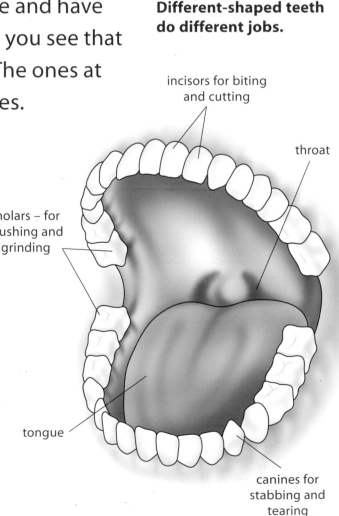

Different-shaped teeth do different jobs.

incisors for biting and cutting

throat

molars – for crushing and grinding

tongue

canines for stabbing and tearing

At the back of your mouth are wide, blocky teeth called molars. These are for chewing your food and grinding it up.

As you chew, your tongue rolls the food around in your mouth, pushing it towards your molars so they can crush it. At the same time, a watery liquid builds up in your mouth and mixes with the food. The liquid is called spit, or saliva. It helps to soften your food and turn it into a mash.

Humans have two sets of teeth in their lifetime. There are 20 teeth in the first set. As you grow up these fall out and are replaced by the second set. By the time you are an adult you should have 32 teeth.

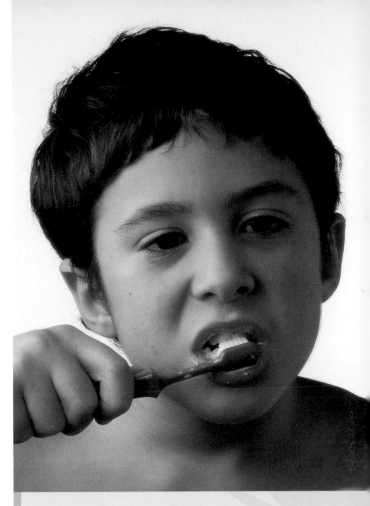

Tooth attack

As you bite and chew food, tiny bits of it stick to your teeth and are left behind when you swallow. Germs live on these bits of old food and over time they attack your teeth and make them rot. Keep your teeth healthy by cleaning them at least twice a day with a toothbrush and toothpaste.

Down the food pipe

When the food in your mouth is soft enough to swallow, it slides down your throat into your food pipe.

Another name for the food pipe is the oesophagus. The oesophagus is next to your windpipe, which you use to breathe. Both tubes are connected to the back of your throat. When you swallow food, a flap of skin called the epiglottis automatically covers the top of your windpipe so that the food does not go down the wrong way and choke you. If food gets into your windpipe, you have to cough to push it back out again.

When you swallow food it slides down your oesophagus.

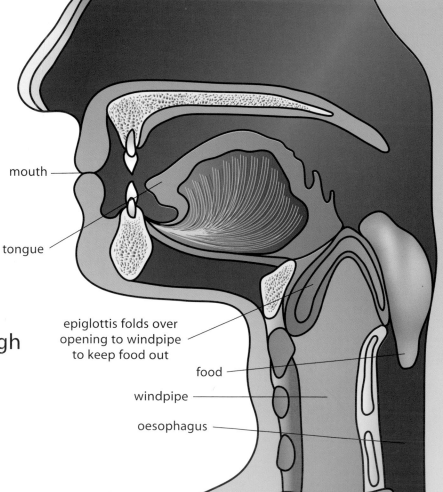

mouth

tongue

epiglottis folds over opening to windpipe to keep food out

food

windpipe

oesophagus

The oesophagus is a soft, stretchy tube about 25 centimetres long and as thick as your thumb. Muscles in the walls of the tube squeeze together behind the mouthful of food, pushing it along. As the food moves forward, the next set of muscles squeezes and pushes it further along.

Your oesophagus moves food automatically, without you making it happen. If it did not, the food would just stay where it was. The muscles make it possible for food to travel 'down' your oesophagus even if you are standing on your head – although it is not comfortable or safe to try eating in this way!

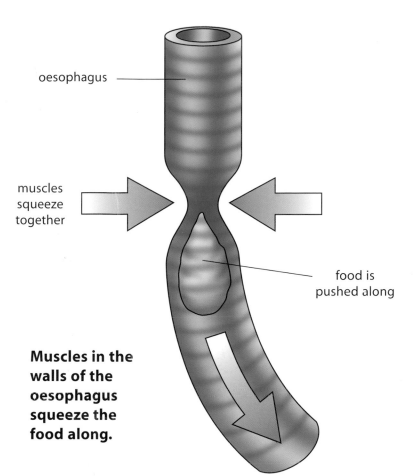

oesophagus

muscles squeeze together

food is pushed along

Muscles in the walls of the oesophagus squeeze the food along.

Letting out air

Whenever you eat, you swallow air with your food. Sometimes the air comes back up the oesophagus as a belch. Gas can also come out at the other end of your digestive system. This gas, or wind, is made by friendly bacteria that live in your intestines.

Into the stomach

A mouthful of food takes about six seconds to travel down your oesophagus. Then the mashed-up mouthful is pushed into the stomach.

Your stomach is just under your ribs. It is where your digestive tube becomes like a stretchy bean-shaped bag. Food collects in the stomach and stays there for about one to four hours depending on what you have eaten. The walls of the stomach are made of muscles that squeeze and churn the food over and over, breaking it down into a thick, soupy liquid.

Meat and oily or fatty foods, such as chips, take longer to break down in the stomach than other foods.

At the same time, special liquids called gastric juices leak out of the stomach walls to help dissolve the food. These juices are so strong that they kill off most germs, or harmful bacteria, that you may have eaten with the food. Bacteria are invisibly small living things that exist all around us and some of them can make us ill.

At the bottom of the stomach is a tight ring of muscles that acts as a gateway. When the food is ready to move on, the gateway opens and shuts, squirting the food a bit at a time into the next part of the digestive system – the small intestine.

Snaky stomach

After swallowing a large meal, such as a deer or a crocodile, a big snake will not need to eat again for a week or more.

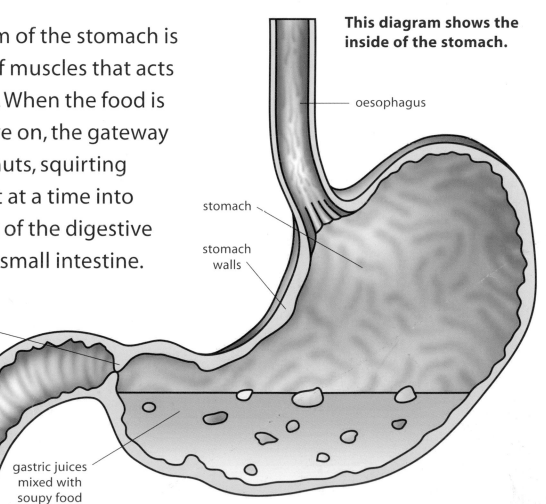

This diagram shows the inside of the stomach.

oesophagus

stomach

stomach walls

gateway to small intestine

gastric juices mixed with soupy food

Along the small intestine

In the small intestine, the nutrients in food are separated out and sent to the rest of the body. But first of all the mushy soup from the stomach has to be turned into a thin liquid.

The small intestine is called 'small', but it is about as wide as a tube of toothpaste and over six metres long. It is bundled up so tightly that it fits into a space inside your body that is smaller than a football. The small intestine has muscles in its walls and these squeeze the food along in a similar way to the oesophagus.

The small intestine is folded up underneath the stomach.

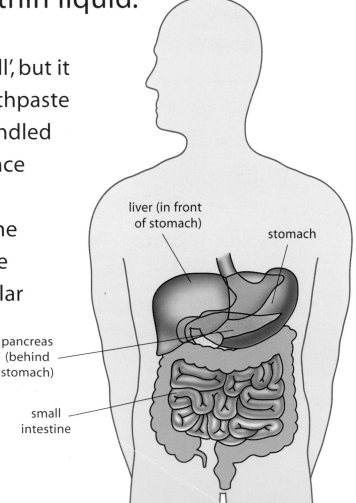

liver (in front of stomach)

stomach

pancreas (behind stomach)

small intestine

As the food moves along, it mixes with more digestive juices that carry on breaking it up. These juices come from the liver, the pancreas and the walls of the small intestine. They dissolve the bits of food that the gastric juices did not break up.

After about one to six hours, the food in the small intestine has become a watery liquid full of invisibly small nutrients and other food bits. The nutrients are so small that they can soak through the walls of the small intestine into tiny tubes, called blood vessels, inside the walls. Here, they mix with the blood inside the vessels and are taken to the liver.

See for yourself

Blood lines

Your body is full of thousands and thousands of tubes called blood vessels. They carry blood to almost every part of your body. Some blood vessels are bigger than others. You can usually see some of the thicker ones as faint blue lines on the inside of your wrists. Blood is pumped through the blood vessels by your heart.

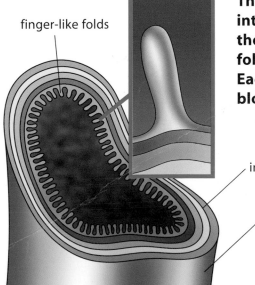

finger-like folds

The wall of the small intestine is lined with thousands of tiny folds, like fingers. Each 'finger' contains blood vessels.

intestine wall

small intestine

Through the liver

Your liver is like a guard that stands between your digestive system and the rest of your body. It balances and checks the nutrients and other chemicals in your blood.

Everything that goes into your blood is brought to the liver to be checked, sorted and sometimes stored. Nutrients that your body needs are put back into your blood and carried to the rest of your body to be used. If your body does not need all the nutrients straight away, the liver stores some of them for later.

An adult's liver weighs about 1.5 kilogrammes.

Small blood vessels in the intestine feed into a larger blood vessel that brings the blood to the liver. Another blood vessel then takes the treated blood to the heart.

The liver also protects your body from anything harmful or poisonous that you might have swallowed. Harmful chemicals in the blood, such as drugs or alcohol, are filtered out by the liver and then changed to make them harmless.

Your liver also makes a liquid called bile. Bile is one of the digestive juices sent to the small intestine to help break down food. Bile is especially good at breaking up fat. It is stored next to the liver in a small bag, called the gall bladder, until it is needed.

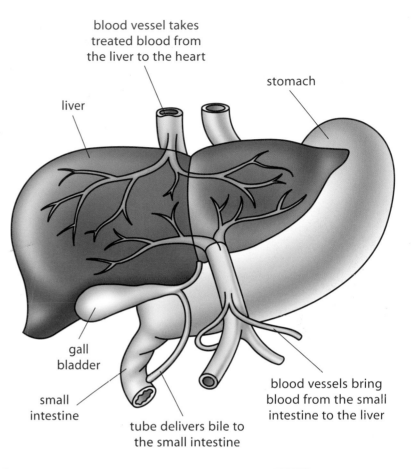

blood vessel takes treated blood from the liver to the heart

stomach

liver

gall bladder

small intestine

tube delivers bile to the small intestine

blood vessels bring blood from the small intestine to the liver

Liver damage

Beer, cider, wine and drinks such as whisky, vodka and gin contain a poisonous chemical called alcohol. When people drink alcohol their liver filters out most of the poison and makes it less harmful. However, this process damages the liver, and can eventually stop it from working altogether.

Around the body

The blood that leaves your liver is loaded up with nutrients to be delivered to all the parts of your body that need them.

Your body is made up of millions of tiny pieces called cells. Blood vessels carry blood to all the cells in your body and each cell takes the nutrients it needs out of the blood.

Your cells use different nutrients in different ways. There are three main types of nutrients in food – carbohydrates, protein and fats. Carbohydrates give you energy. Bread, rice, pasta, potatoes and sugary foods all contain lots of carbohydrates.

Carbohydrates are easy for the body to digest and turn into energy. Athletes often build up their energy by eating carbohydrates such as pasta.

Vitamin C is found in fruit and vegetables, especially oranges, tomatoes and green vegetables. It helps to fight off illness and heal wounds.

Protein builds new cells and mends damaged ones. Protein comes from meat, fish, eggs, milk, cheese, beans and nuts. Fats also give you energy and they help with the growth of some cells. Fats are found in meat, oils, butter, milk, cheese and chocolate.

Food also contains chemicals called vitamins and minerals. There are lots of different vitamins and minerals and our bodies need most of them every day to keep us strong and healthy. Many vitamins and some minerals are found in fresh fruit and vegetables. Calcium is an important mineral found in milk. Iron, another mineral, is found in fish and red meat.

Drinking water

To go on working, your body needs lots of water as well as food. Your body loses water every day, when you breathe out, sweat and go to the toilet. To replace the water you lose, you need to drink as much as eight glasses of water a day!

Out of the large intestine

Not all of the food you eat goes into your blood. Some of it is left behind in the small intestine. This is called waste matter.

Waste matter is food that cannot be broken up into small enough pieces to pass into the blood, or it is something that the body cannot use. When waste matter reaches the end of the small intestine it is pushed into the last part of the digestive system – the large intestine.

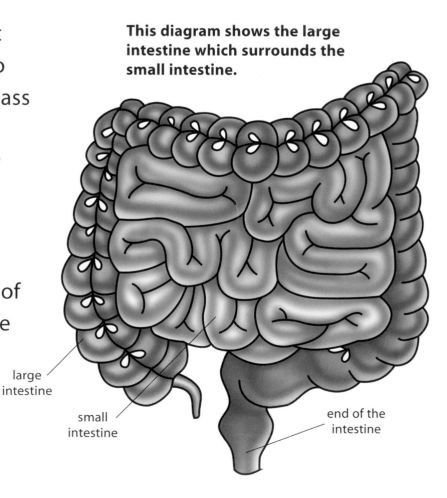

This diagram shows the large intestine which surrounds the small intestine.

large intestine

small intestine

end of the intestine

Fruit and vegetables have lots of tough, stringy material in them called fibre. Fibre makes it easier for waste matter to travel through your large intestine.

The large intestine is a shorter, wider tube that wraps around the small intestine. It is about 1.5 metres long and almost as wide as your fist. Billions of bacteria live in your large intestine. Most of them are 'friendly bacteria' because they help to break down some of the last bits of really tough food. They also help to protect your body from other, unfriendly bacteria.

At first the waste matter is a runny, watery liquid. As it moves along the large intestine most of the water soaks through the walls and into your blood. The waste matter gradually gets thicker and more solid all the time, until at last it reaches the end of your intestine and leaves your body as poo.

Wash your hands

Over half your poo is made of bacteria from your large intestine. These bacteria are helpful inside your intestine, but if passed from your hands to your mouth they can make you ill. That is why it is important to wash your hands after going to the toilet.

Keeping a balance

Our bodies are different shapes and sizes, and we use them in different ways. So although we all need the same kinds of nutrients to stay healthy, the amount we need is special to each of us.

It is important to give your body all of the nutrients, vitamins and minerals it needs. This means eating lots of different foods, rather than always eating the same few things. But it is also important to put the right amount of food into your body.

It is better to eat lots of vegetables, fruits and starchy carbohydrates such as brown bread and rice, and only small amounts of fatty or sugary foods such as doughnuts and cakes.

If you eat more food than you need, the nutrients you do not use are stored in your body as fat (inside fat cells) for later. If you go on eating too much you build up more fat and become overweight. Your heart and other muscles have to work hard to keep your body working, and some parts of your body will wear out more quickly.

If you do not eat enough, your body will be starved of some of the nutrients it needs. This may mean that your bones or muscles do not grow properly. You may get tired quickly, and will be more likely to catch illnesses. A good diet is all about finding the right balance for your body.

Winter stores

Penguins and polar bears build up large stores of fat in their bodies during the summer. When winter comes, the fat keeps them warm and gives them energy when they cannot find any other food.

Your body cannot store protein, so you need to eat some every day. This does not always mean eating meat or fish. Cheese, nuts and beans are all great sources of protein.

Looking after your body

We have to eat to stay alive, but sometimes foods can do us harm and even kill us.

Foods that are pre-cooked and sold ready to eat from packages and tins may have lots of extra chemicals in them to make them look and taste nice. If we eat too much of this kind of food, these chemicals can build up inside our bodies and make us ill.

Sugary foods and drinks leave behind a sticky paste that attacks your teeth. It is best not to eat too many of them and to make sure you brush your teeth afterwards.

If you eat food that is infected by germs or is mouldy or 'bad', it can make you very ill. You cannot see germs and it is not always easy to tell when food has gone bad, so it is important to keep food clean and to cook it properly. Make sure your hands are clean before you touch food. Wash raw fruit and vegetables before you eat them. Keep food covered to keep flies away, and always put leftovers in a fridge.

Some people's bodies do not like certain foods. A particular food may make them sick or give them a skin rash, or even make it hard for them to breathe. This is known as a food allergy. People can be allergic to any sort of food, especially milk, eggs, wheat, nuts or shellfish.

Food that is left lying around for too long starts to look wrinkled or bruised. Sometimes green or white fuzzy-looking patches grow on it – this is called mould. Old food should be thrown away.

See for yourself

Growing mould

Leave a piece of fruit or bread on a plate in a corner of the kitchen and watch what happens to it. After several days it should start to go mouldy. Mould is spread by tiny cells that float in the air until they find somewhere to land and grow.

Body words

Words shown in italics, *like this*, are a guide to how a particular word sounds.

Bacteria
Invisibly small living things that exist all around us and inside our bodies. Some are helpful to us and some are harmful.

Bile
A liquid made in the liver and sent to the small intestine to help break down food.

Blood vessels
The network of tubes that carries blood to every part of your body.

Carbohydrate *(kar-bo-hi-drate)*
A type of nutrient that gives you energy.

Cells
Tiny bits of living material from which all of the parts of your body are built. There are many different types of cell in your body.

Diet
The type and mixture of foods that you eat on a regular basis.

Digestion *(dye-jes-chun)*
Breaking up food into tiny pieces so that the body can use the nutrients in it.

Digestive system
The parts of your body that work to break down and digest your food. The main parts of the digestive system include your mouth, oesophagus, stomach, liver, pancreas and intestines.

Epiglottis *(eh-pih-gloh-tiss)*
A flap of skin in your throat that covers the entrance to the windpipe when you swallow food.

Fat
A type of nutrient that gives you energy and helps to grow cells.

Gastric juice
A liquid in the stomach that helps to break down food.

Intestines
A long, stretchy tube that carries food from your stomach to your bottom. It has two parts: the small intestine and the large intestine.

Minerals
A group of chemicals found in food that helps to keep the body healthy.

Nutrients *(new-tree-ants)*
The parts of food that the body needs in order to work properly, for example, to give us energy and to build and repair cells.

Oesophagus *(uh-sof-fuh-gus)*
The stretchy tube that carries food from your mouth to your stomach.

Protein
A type of nutrient that helps your body to grow and repair itself.

Saliva
The watery liquid in your mouth that helps to soften food as you chew it.

Vitamins
A group of chemicals found in food that helps to keep the body healthy.

Waste matter
Food, dead cells and bacteria that the body cannot use.

Windpipe
A tube that carries air from your mouth and nose to your lungs when you breathe in.

Body facts

- An adult makes about one litre of saliva a day – enough to fill three cans of cold drink.

- When your stomach is empty it is about as big as your fist. If you filled it up, it would stretch to hold as much as four to six drinking glasses full of food and liquid.

- Waste matter can take up to 20 hours or more to travel through the large intestine.

- There are about 400 different types of bacteria in the large intestine.

Index